Lilt in the Mountains

"What is a poem? It is a window into the valley of a poet's mind."

Lilt in the Mountains

A Volume of Verse

by

Monroe Thomas

(April 3, 1903–February 10, 1957)

Dedication

To Dr. A.E. Gouge
A lover of humanity
...and my friend and physician

_____

In his early attempt in 1942 to publish Lilt, *Monroe had planned a dedication page to Dr. A.E. Gouge. Dr. Gouge exemplified the best of those physicians who chose to deliver quality care to those who live and work in frontier outposts. He and Monroe established a close relationship over the long course of Monroe's intractable illness, and Dr. Gouge diligently searched for possible treatments, sending Monroe to several different hospitals over the years. Unfortunately, there was no cure to be found, but Monroe deeply valued Dr. Gouge's efforts, encouragement, and care.*

CONTENTS

Signs and Seasons

Nature

Life and Death

FOREWORD

Excerpted and adapted from the original version of Lilt in the Mountains

Three years after the turn of the twentieth century, Monroe Thomas was born on a small mountain farm located on Gouge's Creek near Spruce Pine, N.C., the third child in a family of seven. As it was for many mountain families of that time, survival was precarious and depended upon hard work, not only of the parents, but also of the offspring. His father, Alpheus H. Thomas, worked on the railroad and was often forced to be away from home, leaving his mother, Maggie, to do outside work in the forests and fields with the older boys. It is a testament to their labors and industriousness that they raised all seven of their children to adulthood.

Monroe was a precocious child, walking and talking at just nine months of age. About this time, left in the care of older brothers by his mother who was working outside, he fell into an open fire burning on the hearth. His head and right hand were burned so badly that he bore the scars of this accident all his life. In retrospect, this early injury seemed to have been a grim harbinger of all the physical ills that he would be compelled to suffer throughout his lifetime. Early in his childhood, Monroe suffered a near fatal case of typhoid. He was then struck down by osteomyelitis, a rare and serious infection of the bone, which reoccurred with life-threatening attacks at unpredictable intervals for the rest of his life. The disease crippled him and ultimately caused his death.

His increasingly severe physical problems limited his opportunity to attend school. Between bouts of illness, he managed to attend elementary school for four terms (the length of the

Mitchell County term in the early 1900s was 55 days, and was often broken down into two equal parts, one before and one after the harvest to allow children to help with farm work). Monroe took it upon himself to learn the rest of the elementary subject matter at home. During a remission of the disease at age sixteen, he entered Yancey Collegiate Institute at Burnsville, N.C. as a high school freshman. He amazed his high school teachers by the ease with which he mastered the high school subject matter, and three years later, he graduated as valedictorian of his class. Ever afterwards he remembered those years as the happiest of his life. The only other formal education that he had was one year of Teacher Training at Bakersville, N.C.

Few people who knew Monroe would dispute that he was in many ways a unique and outstanding person. Part of this may have been due to the fact that he, in essence, was truly a self-educated person. Unfettered by the constraints of a prescribed curriculum as a child and limited in physical activity by his illnesses, his mind was free to search and learn. Despite his lack of formal schooling, he undoubtedly was one of the better educated persons of his day. He read widely in many of the academic fields: literature, philosophy, history, psychology, religion, mathematics, and the sciences. Not only did he know a great deal about these subjects, he seemed to have identified himself vicariously with the writers and their lives to such an extent that he almost became a partner with them.

Monroe possessed a very analytical mind, and in some ways was a mathematical prodigy. He studied math without the benefit of a teacher and developed an understanding of the subject that centered on reducing complex problems to simple terms. He had an intense curiosity about how things worked, and enjoyed working on neighbors' typewriters and tinkering with clocks of all sorts. He also learned the Morse code during a brief stint as assistant postmaster in the Kona Depot. He befriended an agent there, and together they ran a telegraph line connecting their houses so they could practice the code.

Monroe was a master teacher even though he was only able to teach formally for six terms. For him, the school day had no end. After school hours, on Saturdays, Sundays, and holidays, children gathered back at the school to listen and to participate in the readings that he conducted. It was here that many barefoot children got their first glimpse into the wonderful world of literature. After he became too ill to oversee a classroom, he taught his young niece Jo Ann how to read, write, and do arithmetic during a time when she was staying with the family. He used the same imagination and care in tailoring the material to fit the needs of this one student as he had in planning for his classes.

Monroe enjoyed contact with a variety of people. Kona was the junction between the CC&O and Black Mountain Railroads, and he met many different people and made many friends. During his illnesses, he had a host of visitors: the young mountain students who sought help with school problems, the local educators who wanted his views on methods of education, the occasional writers who drifted by to look over his work, and the neighbors who came by just to sit and talk. He particularly enjoyed engaging his visitors in heated discussions of the merits of consolidation of neighborhood schools or the merits of a particular Shakespearean play, but he was also interested in listening to local history. He developed several family histories and genealogical charts for the Thomas, Silver, and Robinson families, and was proud of the rich heritage of the mountain people. He was a deeply religious man, tolerant in his judgment of his fellow man. From his thorough study and reading he knew the Bible as few others did, and held a nightly devotion for the family members.

His mountain surroundings were an integral part of his life, and so long as he was able, he took long walks every day. He observed the majestic peaks of the Black Mountain Range that surrounded his home, and noted their changing aspects with the seasons and weather. He knew every nook and corner of the outdoors—every plant, every bird, every form of life—and felt himself a part of nature. To him, all life had value—the solitary wild rose blooming on the hillside no more nor less than the pampered flower blooming in the hot house. His deep feelings of kindred to and awareness of all parts of nature are reflected in his poetry.

As the pages of this book will show, Monroe possessed the soul and the insight of a poet. With a degree of sadness, one wonders what his accomplishments might have been had fate been kinder to him. His subject matter was gleaned from the mountainous environment in which he lived and from the customs and modes of life practiced by his people—relatives and neighbors. Because of his invalidism he was unable to actively participate in the physical operation of his family's small farm, but he nevertheless took an active interest in everything that was going on. Monroe's isolation was only physical; his mind seemed free of all bounds, was never pent up, and roamed the universe over. I am honored to have been his brother.

Walter Thomas, Spruce Pine, N.C., 1985

PREFACE

My high school English teacher, Miss Frances McMath, first led me to understand and love poetry. She taught that poetry is beautiful and that every object in nature is a poem, beautiful or otherwise according to how we read and interpret it. Under the influence of her teaching I came out of high school in 1924 with my mind open to the beauties of nature around me, and this little book which I call *Lilt in the Mountains*, written through the years that followed, is the result. In it I have not tried to teach any lessons, or at least not many, nor have I written for profit or fame but simply for the joy of it and to preserve for future use my reactions to the beauty of the passing moment.

Writing *Lilt in the Mountains* has given me great happiness, and I hope that you who read it will find in it a happiness as great as has been mine. I believe you will, but even if your joy is only partly as great, we both will have been amply rewarded—you for the reading and I for the writing.

Although a slender volume, *Lilt in the Mountains* has been many years in the making, almost a score. Yet how well I remember the writing of every poem and the circumstances that called it into being! Some of the poems were written for children, others for grownups, but all for the joy of putting my thoughts and feelings into expression. The very first of all was "Song to the Sun," an accomplishment that filled me with great pleasure and hope. Then came "Moonlight," followed by "My Magic Tree," and on down to "Farmer Joe," the very last of all though that is not the order they are given in the book. None sprang into being fullgrown, but all grew from lowly beginnings and were written many times over in the efforts to make them express more accurately my thoughts and feelings. I have ever believed that the beauty of an idea lies chiefly in its manner of expression, and for this reason I have never grown weary of searching for the right word. As a result, my poems have remained fluid up until the present, and will become crystalized now only because of publication.

However, I have never striven for form, unless simplicity of expression be accounted as such. Indeed, I know almost next to nothing about the composition of formal verse, and have no doubt but that *Lilt in the Mountains* will be found wanting, weighed by its standards. Instead, my strivings have all been to express the music of my thoughts and feelings simply and truthfully, and to combine them in such a way as to give the most pleasing picture.

In order to illustrate my meaning let me take you briefly into my workshop. In the poem "To a Wild Rose," the line reading "For the wild bird and ant and bee" at one time read, "For singing bird and buzzing bee." According to the rules of scansion, as I understand them, the second is a better line than the first. But it doesn't express fully the thought and feeling I wanted to convey; namely, the happiness of having discovered that the wild rose was created for all of nature to have and enjoy equally. But this discovery didn't come all at once, but grew with a gradual unfolding, and since "singing" and "buzzing" are limiting words, they became undesirable as my inspiration developed. What I wanted was an all-inclusive expression, one that would leave the imagination in an expanding rather than in a contracting mood. Therefore I changed the line to read as it does in the first instance, adding the word "wild" to heighten the feeling of freedom which I wished the poem to express. And although this latter word makes the measure irregular, both it and the other changes I believe are for the best, and add greatly to the beauty and effectiveness of the line.

Another irregularity in this same poem, judged by formal standards, is found in the last line: "beauty" is not given a rhyme. At one time the poem contained a line ending in the word "duty" to remedy this defect. But later as my thoughts and feelings developed, I saw that this wouldn't do, for any word even suggestive of duty became repellent to my growing idea of the wild rose as a glad, free gift to all. So I cut it out, and as I couldn't find another rhyme for "beauty" that would expand rather tham cramp my meaning, I left the line out entirely. Under the circumstances I believe the value and beauty of the poem as a whole is enhanced rather than marred by the omission.

There is one other thing I wish to say in connection with the development of the poems in *Lilt in the Mountains*. It is this: I have ever found in nature, in all her forms and phenomena, a friend. In flower and bird and sunset I find more than the bodily eye and ear record. I find a spiritual kinship, a relationship deeper than the physical, and feel that underneath the surface we all belong to the same great unity, the brotherhood of life and creation. It is in the light of this understanding, although I have not stated it anywhere in specific words, that I have endeavored to develop my work.

Thus have the poems of *Lilt in the Mountains* been nurtured from their lowly beginnings to their present forms. It has been a work of infinite joy. However, I hope their growth will not stop here, but will continue in other hands than mine. For I hope as you read you will say: "According to my reaction of this same experience, the author could have improved this expression by saying it this way..." In this way the poems will become your very own, and that is the spirit in which I pass them to you.

Now as I reread my poems and live again the scenes they bring to mind, having been forced indoors and removed from the source of my inspiration by illness, I find that reward enough, and if others too can get enjoyment from them, I shall count it a greater reward still.

Monroe Thomas, Kona, N.C., October 1946

———————————————————————

It was at this time in 1946 that Monroe began to seek publication of *Lilt in the Mountains*. One letter to a prospective publisher contained the following information:

> *All of the poems are original and none of them have ever been published in any form, except one, the short poem entitled "Fall," which appeared in the Sunday edition of* The Asheville Citizen *in 1937. Many of them, however, have been read over radio station WPTF in Raleigh by announcer Phil Ellis, but in my agreement with Mr. Ellis, I retained complete ownership of the poems.*
>
> *I am making the submission blindly, knowing nothing about the conditions under which you make publication. Also, this is the first time I have ever submitted material to a publisher and I know not whether I have the manuscript in the right form. I know it should have been typewritten, but being crippled in my arms, I am unable to type it and haven't the means to get it done, so I have printed it as legibly as I could by hand. I hope none of these things will detract from your consideration of the poems themselves.*

Monroe continued to work, albeit unsuccessfully, to have the *Lilt* manuscript published in its entirety, but only a handful of the poems were ever printed, primarily in *Our State* magazine and local newspapers. Throughout his relatively short life he continued to draft, revise, and polish his poetry. While his poems were written with the simplicity of local language and reflect the values of his time and place, they offer the reader an honest and insightful view into the mind of an exceptional man. This truly was the passion of his life.

Jo Ann Thomas Croom, Mars Hill, N.C., December 2017

ACKNOWLEDGMENTS

Even in the face of unrelenting and progressive illness, Monroe Thomas was able to lead a productive and fulfilling life because he had the willing support of his family and friends. His primary health caregivers throughout his long struggle were members of his immediate family—primarily his brothers, Clayton and Robah Thomas, and his sister, Savannah Thomas Duncan. Equally important were those family members and friends who gave him encouragement for his work through their visits, gifts, conversations, and letters.

After his death, many people, some of whom had not known Monroe personally, worked to see that his written legacy was preserved and honored. Among these were Malcom Ross, who featured Monroe in a 1958 *National Geographic* article about the Toe River Valley region; Michael Joslin, Jodi Higgins, and Elizabeth Hunter, all regional authors who wrote about Monroe in local publications; Everett Kivette and Susan Larson, who were instrumental in the Toe River Arts Council Readers' Theatre production of *The Gentle Giant of Kona* that showcased the essence of Monroe's life and art; and C. Robert Jones, playwright.

The organization and compilation of this current volume of Monroe's poetry took place thanks to the efforts of these dedicated people: Pauline Cheek assisted in preliminary editing; Elizabeth Hunter compiled the collections of Monroe's many revisions; and Noel Kinnamon used his poetic expertise to select suitable examples from Monroe's myriad revisions. More recently, Kathleen Croom Beck, Monroe's great niece, transcribed both Monroe's poems and journal entries from their original handwritten brown notebooks and contributed graphic illustrations; Jo Ann Thomas Croom, Monroe's niece, pursued the effort to finally put her uncle's poems into a professionally printed volume; and Maggie Powell provided assistance with editing, design, and print production.

INTRODUCTION

The brief formal exposure to poetry that Monroe experienced as a high school student seemingly liberated an inner core of expression that had been largely dormant until that time. It is difficult to imagine that his childhood afforded much opportunity for exposure to poetry, though his father, Pa, would occasionally recite a poem on the front porch of their home—one that he had memorized as a boy for a program of entertainment at his school. The poem was an account of how a young man, tired of his life at home, had come to sea, and on his first voyage had been shipwrecked and lost in a storm. I can imagine the hush that must have fallen over the small audience of hard-working and tired members of the community as he recited with dramatic effect the troubles and travails of the unfortunate young man that ended with the refrain, "Oh sailor boy! Oh sailor boy! Peace to thy soul."

Pa's recitation of the poem so many years later on that front porch suggests that his initial dramatic rendition at entertainment night must have been a highlight of his school experience. In a similar way, perhaps it impacted Monroe in a profound way as one of his early exposures to the joys of poetry.

Monroe starting writing poetry in earnest in 1924, basing much of his material on his surroundings: nature, and his community of relatives and neighbors. As with all of his endeavors, Monroe was meticulous about his poetry. Some of his journal entries describe the detailed process he went through as he revised and polished his work. The following entry outlines the persistent attention he paid to achieving a product that reflected his vision of what the poem should be.

April 12, 1942: I've been working on my book of rhymed, formal verse during the past week, revising, correcting, smoothing. This is my great joy, the balm of my life. I'm a great stickler for the right word, and I never tire of searching for it to gain the effect or feeling that I wish to produce. The charm in verse of this kind lies, I think, in the impression it makes on the mind or spirit (whichever you will), and the use of the right word or combination of words is all-important. As finally corrected I made my poem read like this.

Burn, Kindly Fire
Burn, kindly fire, burn, warmly burn.
Outside the cold winds howl and blow,
And every leaf and twig and fern
Is deeply hid beneath the snow.

Burn, kindly fire, burn, brightly burn,
And fill our room with warmth and glow
While every leaf and twig and fern
Lies deeply hid and cold winds blow.

Let me take you into my workshop, show you the changes I made, and tell you why I made them. Then you may judge for yourself whether they are for the better or not. The unrevised version read:

Burn, kindly fire, warmly burn.
Outside the cold winds howl and blow,
And every leaf and fern
Is deeply hid beneath the snow.

Burn, kindly fire, brightly burn,
And fill our room with tender glow,
While, outside, leaf and fern
Lie deeply hid and cold winds blow.

You'll notice that the first line of each revised stanza has the word "burn" added, and that the third lines have "and twig," thus making all the lines of the same poetical length. This was done to secure more harmony and smoothness, and I think it has also added to the feeling I wished to produce, one of security and warmth amid the storm. The change made in the third line of the second stanza, taking out "outside" and making it read like its corresponding line in the first stanza except for the initial word, was done for the same reason, to get more smoothness and harmony of feeling.

The feeling, security amid storm, is the main thing that I wish to convey—internal warmth and cheerfulness and peace while the storm rages around. I did everything I could to increase the contrast. That is why I added the word "twig," to make the storm's grip all the more inclusive on the outside as it holds everything prisoner, and the word "warmth" in the second stanza to increase the feeling of security and well-being in the room, thus heightening the contrast between the outside cold and storm and the inside comfort, although to keep my regular number of feet I had to leave out "tender." However, I think "warmth and glow" a much more expressive phrase than "tender glow," since it conveys the feeling of comfort as well as of light.

But in the poem I wished to convey more than a feeling of physical comfort and warmth in storm—I wanted to produce the deeper feeling of spiritual well-being and safety in the turmoil of destructive forces that beset us on every hand. That's why I changed the third line in stanza two, because I thought the word "outside" when removed increased this effect. How well I have succeeded in conveying this I can't say, but what I've striven to do is to make you see a physical picture, but feel a deeper spiritual reaction. That's why I sought to increase the contrast between the snow and wind outside and the security of the room, warmed and cheered by the kindly fire.

The poems included in this collection are divided into broad categories indicative of the world Monroe lived in and wrote about—broadly speaking, the relationships he had with nature and people close to him. In most cases, each poem is followed by a brief explanation by Monroe, describing what influenced him to write that particular piece.

My uncle was very thorough in all of his endeavors, always striving for clarity and precision. Though with his poetry, his ultimate goal was that his readers enjoy his words, and be inspired to further creativity from them. In the brief period when I was five years old and staying Down Home (the home where my grandparents raised their children and still lived, along with Monroe), Monroe took it upon himself to begin my education. In addition to having regular school time for reading and writing and arithmetic, he began to instill an appreciation for poetry by including some children's poems for me to memorize. One that I remember was a simple little ditty, but one that has a deeper meaning for those who look closely.

> *Little drops of water,*
> *Little grains of sand,*
> *Make the mighty ocean,*
> *And the pleasant land.*

When I had learned it sufficiently, Monroe had me recite it to the family that daily gathered in the living room for after-supper discussion and devotion. He genuinely believed that to be fully appreciated, poetry should be spoken aloud, not just silently read. It is in this speaking and hearing that the true message can be felt and experienced over time and beyond place.

Jo Ann Thomas Croom, Mars Hill, N.C., September 2017

Love

To a Friend

When morning's beam, aslant the sky,
     Has raised of light for day a rafter,
And dews are fresh and work is nigh,
     I need the ripple of your laughter,
Your faith and hope, and love held high,
     For now and day that follows after.

When noon rides past and day sinks west,
     And shadows fall across my mind,
And faith is gone, and hope oppressed,
     I need your presence, close and kind,
Your voice, in friendliness caressed,
     Your strength, your courage—all, I find.

When sable robe of evening falls,
     And twilight's beauty bathes the land,
And earth to twinkling star far calls,
     I need the pressure of your hand,
That touch that sweetens all life's galls,
     And tells me still you understand.

To One Lost

In you, I said, I'd found a friend
         Who'd love me well, nor pass me by.
In springtime this; as summer waned
         I swore our love would never die.

I had not learned this lesson well:
         That friendship runs a rapid race;
For now (so soon since then!) I may
         Not hear your voice nor see your face.

To One Unattainable

I find you in the dewdrops;
         I find you in the flowers;
I find you in the moonbeams
         That light in the nightly hours.
I find you in sweet laughter,
         In everything divine.
But what are all my findings worth
         Since you can ne'er be mine?

In love the odds have always been against me. When I was a child learning to walk, I fell in the fire and severely burned my head and hand, causing scars that gave me an irregular baldness and marred my appearance for life. The physical discomforts I suffered from it later were not great, but the self-consciousness was. I had only a little hair left in the middle of the top of my head, where I had clasped my hand, and my family taught me to comb this toward my forehead; but it wouldn't hide the scars, and in itself was unnatural, so that I felt set apart. Yet I was made fun of only a few times. Instead the sympathies were never ending, and always closed with this remark: "He never will be able to get a sweetheart." And this proved true. As a child, I had many sweethearts, whom I loved passionately, tenderly, but none of them would claim me back. However, I was not worried; when I grew up, I said, it would be different. Then, at 13, came the illness which left me a cripple. I did not think of it then as a deterrent to love, but as I grew to manhood I found it was, even more so than my earlier disfigurement and the two together completely sealed me off. The girls I met were kind to me, became friends, and lavished me with admiration; but when I mentioned love they were horrified. Still I loved, for the void in my heart would not be filled in any other way; I loved passionately, violently, but to myself, in silence, not even telling my bosom companion. "To One Unattainable" recounts one of these loves. Only once was there an exception; for one rapturous summer I lived in an idyll of love returned. But presently my loved one was torn from me and never more allowed to come into my presence. "To One Lost" recounts this.

THE CRIPPLE

You scorn me in the city's bright cafés
    When lovely women come to sip their wine;
You jeer me when I stop to watch your plays
    And scoff and say that love will ne'er be mine;
You meet me on the dusky boulevards
    And curse, your grasping arms encircling free
Pale painted forms perfumed with costly nards;
    You pass and mock your demoiselles at me.

Mock on, nor think I want your cheap romance.
    All night she lay with me, her warm flesh curled
Against my crooked side; in love's deep trance
    My life was sealed ere dewy dawn unfurled.
        Fools! not as yours, a common woman free
        For asking, but a virgin princess, she!

———————————————————————

Written long years after I head read Hugo and my memory had grown dim and uncertain. This is my second attempt to write a sonnet.

6

To One Gone Far Away

Now you are gone, the tongues will wag;
They'll sere your life and call you hag,

    And curse the place your form adorns;
With shame they'll weave your pale renown,

    And plait your name with gossip's thorns.

But I, as I go down the years
So full of sorrow's wake of tears,

    May I remember only this:
Long years ago, at even's down,

    You threw me through the dusk a kiss.

HAVE YOU FORGOT

Have you forgot that day, its close?
         The night her ebon shades had drawn
And the moon an ancient goddess rose,
         When you came skipping o'er the lawn.

We found a place beneath the hill
         Where led a moonlit path to guide us,
And there we stopped and all was still,
         And Beauty came and sat beside us.

The silvery moon and all her train
         Shone bright, and softly fell the dew;
And the harp of night sang once again
         An old, old song that's ever new.

We stole from night her magic lute,
         We broke a fragile law, in fine;
And the fruit we took was godly fruit,
         And fair, and sweeter far than wine.

'Twas long and long ago, and May
         Had fled and soon will come December.
Have you forgotten, dear, I say,
         Or do you still, like me, remember?

Mind and Spirit

In the inner gardens of my mind ~ here in these woods ~ my magic tree ~ two idle words ~ contentment

IN THE INNER GARDENS OF MY MIND

In the inner gardens of my mind
  Are things that I have never told
  And shall for aye and ever hold
  As misers hold their hoarded gold.
  And there's a castle old and deep
  Where faery prince and princess sleep
  And king and queen in sorrow keep—
    In the inner gardens of my mind.

In the inner gardens of my mind
  Are paths my friends have never trod
  All set with flowers and hallowed sod
  Where walks at eve my Lord and God.
  And there's a lovely garden dell,
  Fresh watered from a living well,
  Where fondly I am wont to dwell—
    In the inner gardens of my mind.

HERE IN THESE WOODS

Here in these woods amid the vales
      I'll make my bed and lie,
Where rule the winter's howling gales
      And never men pass by;
All lonely I have had to live,
      And lonely let me die;
For life has had no love to give,
      For me no answering cry;
Here let the rains my body seep,
      And summer build a bower
Where none may come, for there's none to weep,
      And none to leave a flower.

Self-pity is the most odious, spirit-deforming, facial-souring evil I know of, and I have ever fought it. Yet it's a comfort most of us like to have around, and once for a short period I gave it free admittance into my heart. It was in 1932 following my first visit to Bakersville after a prolonged absence of nearly two years caused by an attack in my hips. During the previous years I had become attached to a number of friends there, and though none of them kept in touch with me during my illness nor I with them I thought I was missed and would be welcomed back. But when at length I got able to return I found quite the reverse true; none had missed me, and none except my doctor and his wife (to whom this particular rendering of the poems is inscribed) seemed glad to see me back or grieved that my lameness had grown worse. They were not unkind but indifferent, and suddenly I realized my place among them was lost and a feeling of abandonment such as I had never known before seized me. Coming back very melancholic, I gave over during the next few days to an orgy of loneliness and self-pity, and it was then that I wrote the poem "Here in These Woods," which exactly expressed my feelings. But let me say it passed and that afterwards all my friendships had a happy revival.

MY MAGIC TREE

In the garden of my mind there stands
      A magic tree.
Its shadows fall in many lands
      And on every sea,
On the burning desert sands
      And on the verdant lea,
On hills and dales and pleasant vales
      Where the wild bird sings in glee.

And everywhere its shadows stray
      There, too, I'm quickly brought:
To life's grim struggle in the fray
      Where manly deeds are wrought,
To the happy land of laugh and play
      That many in vain have sought,
To wonders true and ever new—
      'Tis thus I live in magic thought.

What my magic tree is in the poem by that name is explained in the last line. I cannot say that the mind is consciousness, but whatever it is I like to think of it other than that, it is as a garden, and of imagination, its power to project and sustain itself in thought, as a tree in that garden; and it was after much pleasant meditation on these likenesses that I wrote my poem. My object was not to teach a lesson, but to make as beautiful a rhyme as I could on the wonders of imagination in this simile, and to make it so simple that a child could understand and appreciate it. Isn't it wonderful, this power God has given us to roam the earth and sky in thought, to go in fancy where we have never been in body? Surely it is one of the things that raise us above the beast and lifts us into the realm of God. But had I wanted to teach a lesson, what a subject this would have been of a mind likened to a garden and thought to a tree! The garden is ours to dress and whether we make it a thing of beauty or a weed patch and the tree of thought one of fruit or thorns depends entirely on us.

My poem was not difficult to write and took but little revising. It gave me much pleasure, but never having received any comment on it I don't know how others like it or whether they understand the thought I was attempting to bring out.

Two Idle Words

I spoke two idle words one day,
Two idle words, an ill and gay,
And sent them out alone to play.
     The first went out in anger hot,
     The next was word by love begot —
Those idle words I spoke one day
And sent out all alone to play.

And then they came again one day,
Those idle words, the ill and gay,
With gifts they'd garnered on the way.
     The first brought back a heart that bled,
     The next a smiling comrade led —
Those idle words I spoke one day
And sent out all alone to play.

_____

I am aware that this type of poem is held in contempt by the aesthetically inclined, but this type meant a great deal to me in my childhood and youth, and the writing of this little poem years later gave me a great thrill and I have ever afterward preserved it.

CONTENTMENT

I've found the world a very pleasant place.

    By day the sun has brought me heat and light,

And nature's lent me food for strength and grace,

    While moon and stars have freed my soul by night.

My neighbors haven't looked on me for wings,

    Nor wished that I was in a hotter clime;

And I've not hunted for the rotten things,

    Nor moaned that I was born out of my time.

"Contentment" was written in answer to those strong, healthy people who go through life moaning at their fate. Surely if moaning were permissible I could qualify. Crippled by a wasting disease at 13, I have hardly had a well day since, with open wounds during all but two years of that time, and, besides, I have sinned and have troubles and financial woes very many. Yet I have not moaned or wished that I was dead or had been born in some other time or place, but on the contrary have enjoyed life to its full. As a foundation to my enjoyment I have loved nature, the warmth and light of the sun, the moon, stars, flowers, rain, snow, wind, and all of it. Next, I have not aspired to high positions, being content with a sufficiency. Last, I have practiced moderation toward my fellow beings. My family and neighbors haven't expected much from me so that what good I have done, however small, has been gain, and I haven't hunted for faults in them but for beauty and kindness and have been rewarded. Truly I can say, "I have found the world a very pleasant place."

SECTION 3

Family and Community

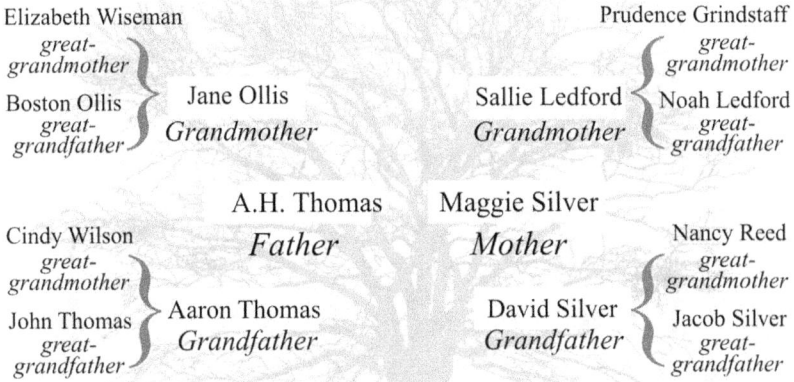

Elizabeth Wiseman
great-grandmother

Boston Ollis
great-grandfather

Jane Ollis
Grandmother

Prudence Grindstaff
great-grandmother

Sallie Ledford
Grandmother

Noah Ledford
great-grandfather

A.H. Thomas
Father

Maggie Silver
Mother

Cindy Wilson
great-grandmother

John Thomas
great-grandfather

Aaron Thomas
Grandfather

David Silver
Grandfather

Nancy Reed
great-grandmother

Jacob Silver
great-grandfather

Monroe

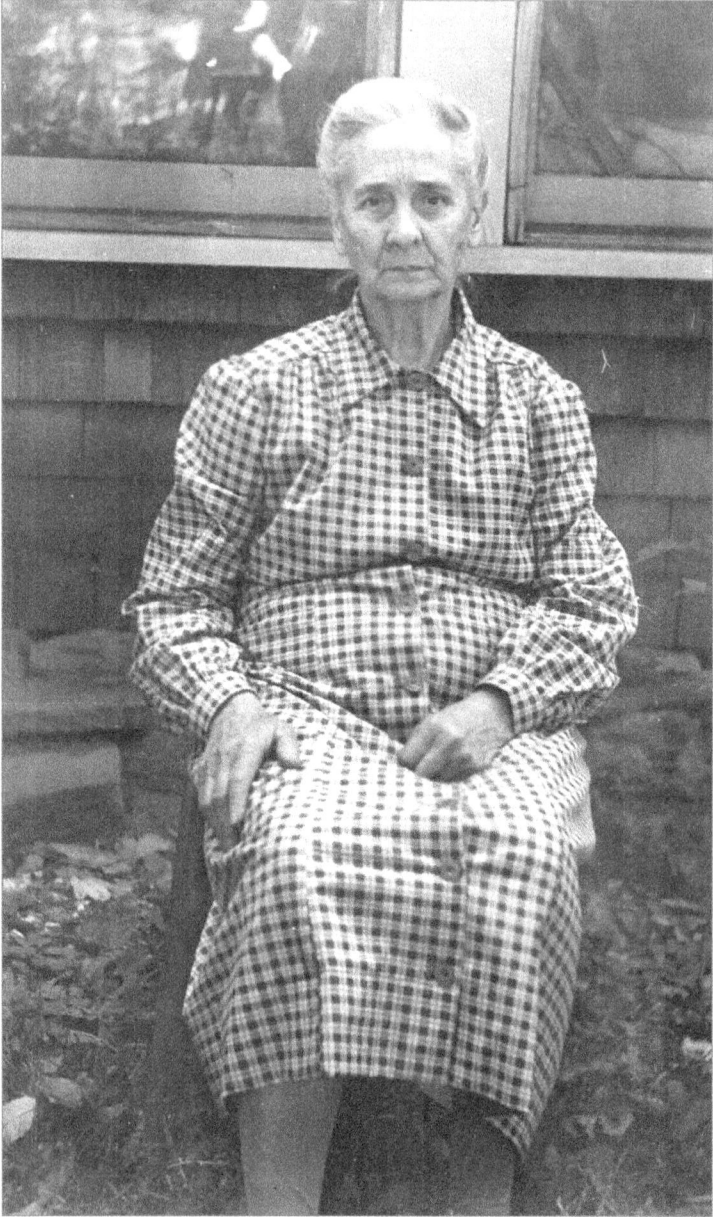

Maggie Silver Thomas, mother of Monroe

To Mother

Time was when beauty lay upon her brow
      Like the dew on hills at morn,
And every rosebud on her boughs
      Bloomed without a thorn.
How fair her dreams, and fairer still her vows,
      When I was born?

Alas! for faded now are all her roses;
      Faded, too, her youthful dreams.
But on her brow a fairer bloom reposes
      Than were ever girlish gleams:
The purity her motherhood discloses
      And her faded hope redeems.

Jane Ollis Thomas, paternal grandmother of Monroe

GRANDMA

Grandma is old and wrinkled and gray,
Past fourscore and five.
She sits in the sun all day long
In her little old rickety chair,
Her closest companion,
And coughs and squints her eyes,
And knits and knits and knits.

Grandma has lost all interest in the living
And never sees us when we pass,
Nor talks nor reads nor anything.
But people come long distances to see her
And bring her oranges and take her picture.
And they tell what a hard life she has lived,
Widowed by a cruel war,
To raise ten boys and four girls
And send them to school
When the country was a wilderness and times were tough
And neighbors were few and far between.
And they walk on tiptoe around her chair,
And talk in hallowed voices and whisper
That her stooped back and bent shoulders
And her knotted hands and twisted fingers
Tell a story...

Sometimes Grandma lays her knitting in her lap,

And adjusting her spectacles with trembling hands,

Looks out over the fields and meadows to the hilly beyond.

And then her dim old eyes fill with tears,

And a strange light glows on her face,

And she gazes long and wistfully

As if she were looking beyond the cattle grazing

And seeing things that are not there now.

But when I ask her what she's thinking about

She jumps and looks at me in a peeved sort of way

And says, "Child, don't make so much noise!"

And goes back to her coughing and squinting,

As she sits in the sun

In her little old rickety chair,

Her closest companion,

And knits and knits and knits.

With this poem begins a number of my attempts at free verse, or what I call free verse, not being very learned in the definition of that term. At least, they are compositions not in conventional form, their poetry being in the thought rather than in words and lines. Yet to make my exact meaning and feeling clear, I chose the words with great care and tried to put rhythm into my phrases. Some might think free verse easily written since it lacks form, but I found it the most difficult of all; in conventional poetry one has aids, such as measure and rhyme, to help bring out the beauty of his subject, but in free verse he has only the thought, which must be good.

"Grandma" and the poem following were drawn from real life, though the characterization of each is of more than one person. "Grandma" is a composite of my paternal grandmother Jane and my maternal step-grandmother Rosanna. The knitting, rugged hands, and hard life belonged to grandmother Jane, but the cough, lack of interest in present surroundings, and impatience with children were grandmother Rosanna's, as were also the home and widowhood (through her first husband, not my grandfather). The individual chair and love of the sun belonged to both, and also the great age, each being in the high nineties when she died. "Grandma" was as I saw them in childhood; as I grew up my picture of them changed, God bless their hearts!

Paternal Grandfather Aaron Thomas, model for Caleb Henson

CALEB HENSON

Caleb Henson was our oldest citizen, a hundred and seven years old when he died.

He was five feet two inches tall, weighed a hundred and twenty pounds in his prime, and wore number five women's shoes.

In winter his door was never shut, and when the weather was fair and he had nothing to do he lay on a bench in the sun.

Married at 35 to a wife half as old as he, he lived on rented land and was kicked about till he was 70, then he bought a farm and settled down.

Henpecked, he pouted instead of talking back and for consolation chewed tobacco and took an occasional dram of whiskey.

But at a hundred his mind was still clear and his eyes undimmed, and he still hoed his corn and chopped his wood and walked a mile and a half to the mill, and his teeth were still white and sound and he never missed a meal.

Caleb carried his country's flag through four years of war and could take up a century and span it with his memory.

Yet he never did anything great, he said, except beget sons and daughters and learn to lie in the sun and live simply, serving merely as a link in one of life's myriad chains.

But we remember him for a few things beside these, to wit:

He hated flies and when he bought his farm and settled
      down he built his house high on a hill, for he had
      observed, he said, that flies are less numerous on a
      hill where the wind blows constantly.

And he screened his windows and doors and made his wife
      a fly swat, and he was the first man in our
      community to dig a pit for his toilet and make it
      flyproof.

He knew the names of the stars and their times and courses,
      having learned them from a companion in the war,
      and was wise in the ways of the fields and woods
      and could tell how a spider spins her web and
      where a wasp stays in winter.

He was a Christian, yet was opposed to our signs and
      beliefs and said that a man's fate depended more on
      his attitude toward life than on how he looked at the
      new moon, and his fortune more on his methods of
      tillage than on the signs of the almanac at planting time.

For these sayings he was roundly denounced, but he stuck
      to his convictions like the bark to a tree and said
      that a man couldn't live a hundred years and not
      learn a few things not writ in the almanac.

Moreover, in his old age he made two poems, although he
      couldn't read and write, never having been to
      school a day in his life, and set them to tunes of his
      own making.

And we learned them and called them "Caleb's Songs,"
      and they can still be heard in our community,
      especially in the springtime.

"Caleb Henson" is an exact reproduction of my grandfather, Aaron Thomas, except for the age, and the "few things besides these," which are of various other men of the community. Grandfather ("Pappy" to his whole family of descendants, grandchildren and all) was only 104 when he died, though his grandfather lived to 107 and his great-grandfather to 114. The "songs," of course, are mine. Because Pappy was a small man we used to jocularly spell his name "big A jumped on little a and mashed out r-o-n." As may be inferred from the characterization, he was a man of unvarying routine, especially in his diet, which he wanted plain with no strange dishes. He liked fried crumbs, bread soup, and coffee, but wouldn't touch stewed potatoes. Once grandmother made some potato soup and he, thinking it was bread soup, was just funneling it down when she happened to call it potato soup; then he pushed his back, and hissing "Ps-s-sht, ps-s-sht!" through his beard, wouldn't touch it again.

He was a sparing talker, not silent but never repeating, and when he grew old, never being sick, he despised being asked over and over how he was. One summer a lumberman lived in the community, and pasturing his cow in Pappy's pasture, had to go by his house to milk. Not knowing Pappy's aversion to this, he began by calling out each morning and evening to know how he was. Pappy answered civilly enough at first, but after a few days he could stand it no longer and the next morning when the lumberman passed and called out, he hissed back, "Ps-s-sht, ps-s-sht! Jist like I was yisterd'y!" After that the man confined his remarks to the weather. Pappy was also a man of vast expectations. When he was ninety years old he got hurt in a mica mine accident and had to be carried to a doctor. The doctor found him hurt seriously—three ribs broken and other grave injuries—but seeing he was an old man, he sought to console him. "You're not hurt bad," he said. "Don't worry, you'll soon be all right." But Pappy wouldn't hear to it. "I reckon I know!" he cried. "Ps-s-sht, ps-s-sht! hit'll take me twenty years to git over it."

CALEB'S SONGS

Number One

Friends and lovers, sleep and rest,

But I have a date on the top of the hill

At the break of the day.

List to the mourning doves—

How they're calling, calling, calling,

And I cannot say them nay!

Friends and lovers, sleep and rest,

But I have a date on the top of the hill

And must up and away.

Number Two

Give me a home on a hill

Where the lightning plays and the storms roar

And the winds sweep;

Where the morning sun first kisses the dew,

And the summer breezes waft the flowers,

And the doves mourn.

Give me a house on a hill

On a hill I know full well

Where the loitering daylight loves to linger

And the night with her lofty train of stars

Swings low.

FARMER JOE

When morning comes and wakes the hills anew,
  And o'er the lakes and streams the mists lie white,
And weeds and webs are dripping wet with dew,
  And robins skip and sing with all their might—
    Then farmer Joe is glad the night is past
    And on the bread of morning breaks his fast.

When morn through noon to evening's westward rolled,
  And hills and clouds lie mirrored in the streams,
And weary bones are glad the day is told,
  And dusk comes up and lights her twinkling gleams,
Then while the birds seek leafy perches deep,
    Joe seeks with night a bed of rest and sleep.

———————————————————————

"Farmer Joe" was begun a long while ago as a poem of four lines and through many revisions brought to its present length and content. I am reminded of an incident that happened in our community. A young mother was counseled by an elderly neighbor woman to pull her baby's nose daily to make it grown long and straight. The young mother was offended; from all appearances, she said, her counselor had pulled her children's noses just a little too much. And so it is with my poems; sometimes I think I have revised them out of all their original beauty and simplicity. But not "Farmer Joe"; as it now stands, it is a poem after my own heart, and farmer Joe is a man I am proud to acknowledge. He lives "far from the maddening crowd," but close to nature and hence to the realities of life. At morning he rises rested, refreshed, and alive to himself and his surroundings; he knows what he wants and needs and greets the day with joy and strength. At evening, though tired, he is still in harmony with himself and his environment, and he knows what has wearied him and what will give him rest. He might well be our ideal; it is not more hurry and tear we need, but more of his spirit and patience.

31

Earth's Cycle

Song To the Sun

You usher in the morn with sparkling dews,

Followed by the sunny noon;

You bring the sunset glow in many hues,

And then the silvery moon.

And countless myriads of twinkling stars

Gleam in all their brilliance dressed

When you withdraw your amber-tinted bars

      To your palace in the west.

Written during the summer of 1924, this was my first permanent poem. Just out of Y.C.I., I wanted to write a great poem, and having chosen my theme, I worked all that summer with my head in the clouds, creating an atmosphere and rhyming images. The difficulty came when I started putting my work together: there was no continuity of thought, and what I finally got out of my summer's exaltation was the above poem of eight lines. Of course I was disappointed, but I later had my reward; for out of the atmosphere and reservoir of images thus built up there came, in time, some of my finest lyrics. My brother Walter called them my "sun poems."

Morning and Evening

Somewhere there is always a rising sun,

    And a morning adorning the world anew;

Somewhere there is always a flame-enkindling east,

    And hills set agleam in the sparkling dew.

Somewhere there is always a setting sun,

    And an evening unrobing the world of light;

Somewhere there is always a twilight-deep'ning west,

    And hills soothed to sleep in the folds of night.

The fact that all the time there is somewhere a morning breaking, and at the same instant somewhere an evening coming has deeply fascinated me and I could not rest until I had written on it. I consider this poem that resulted as the most beautiful of all my poems on this theme, but I was a long time in making it, revising it hundreds of times from its original form (summer of 1926) in the effort to make it harmonize with my concept of the beauty of this wonderful phenomenon. It is also a poem that my friend, Mrs. Ruby Sisk Gouge likes, once quoting it to me in a letter.

A CHILD QUESTIONS THE SUN

O Sun, is there no place where you may rest?
      My mother says when night time comes to me,
And I beneath my soothing sheets lie pressed,
      That you still shine somewhere beyond the sea.

How strange it seems you really never set,
      That in some sky you always have to keep
For children in Japan and far Tibet
      While I with kindly night am fast asleep!

Did God not make for you somewhere a night
      When you have sunk far down behind our west
And brought the moon and stars to give us light?
      O Sun, is there no place where you may rest?

THE SUN REPLIES

All nature wakes with joy when I return
With the kindling light of dawn.
No sooner do my rays begin to burn
      Than in every lot and lawn
Her children wake, a happy, rested throng
      Bathed and freshened in the dew,
And rising, greet me with a shout and song
      And begin their work anew.

From light of dawn till dusky fall of night
      Nature works from pole to pole
And busily absorbs my heat and light
      While the day I westward roll.
She greens the hills and plains and with my beams
      Gives the flowers their tints and hues,
And brings the vapors from the seas and streams
      For the rains and fogs and dews.
I see her from my place up in the sky:
      In her universal plan
The worm he treads upon and passes by
      Has a part the same as man.

Thus nature plans and works the whole day through,
     Stopping not for want nor care;
For there are ever many things to do,
     Be the weather foul or fair.
Not till the shades their shadows eastward throw
     Does she slacken in her toil,
When all her weary children stop and go
     To their homes in leaf and soil.
I linger then a moment with my light
     While she spreads her covers deep
And gently leave her lying down with night
     In the restful robes of sleep.

But on and on I speed across the blue,
     For my work is never done;
My work when it is eve or night to you
     Far away has just begun.
For there is e'er a world in dewdrops dressed
     Waiting for the glorious dawn
And there is e'er a world in some tired west
     Thankful when my light's withdrawn.

"A Child Questions the Sun" and "The Sun Replies" are meant to be in sequence, the first giving the subject, a child's wonder at the sudden revelation that the sun has no resting place, never tarries, never stops, but continues in his work without ceasing, and the second giving an explanation of the phenomenon in terms that the child can understand. I planned to make one poem of them, writing the second, the more difficult, first, but all the while the first intended in my mind as the first stanza; when I got around to doing so a good while later, however, I found myself unable to put it into the same rhyme scheme and so made a separate poem out of it.

In "The Sun Replies" I attempted to show the benign concern of the sun for nature and nature's thankfulness, the industry of the two, and how nature is alike joyous for the dawn and the night, but the work of the sun goes on. During my work I tried to put myself completely in the place and receptive mood of a child and my mind was wonderfully enriched by it.

WHEN I GO OUT IN EVENING'S COOL

When I go out in evening's cool

    What go I out to see?

A streamlet dropping in a pool

    Beside a lilied lea;

A crimson bird in tufted hood

    Asinging merrily;

And darkness lurking in a wood

    To hide both bird and me;

While in the sky, serene and far,

    To set my spirits free,

The night comes bringing in a star—

    That's what I go to see.

When I was able to get out one of my chief delights was in walks, taken mostly at evening and alone. But it was one of the hardest things for my neighbors, and even my family, to understand about me, for our community has few directions in which one can go without being seen; if I felt as they, they said, I would want to sit and rest. There have not been many times since I was thirteen when I have not been physically weary, but still I took my walks, and the little poem, "When I Go Out in Evening's Cool" was written to indicate the reason for them, although it but faintly does so.

NIGHTFALL

The cows stand black against the sky,

    As dusk ascends upon the hill.

From far off comes the lonesome cry,

    Of homing crows, then all is still.

Save two lone crows that downward fly.

    There's not a breeze within the trees,

The mother bird is on her nest,

    And in the sky the candles light,

And dark begins to blot the west.

    Soon now will come the kindly night,

With coverlets of sleep and rest.

I wrote this poem during and following the summer of 1932. The winter before, I had been confined with an attack in my hip to a rolling chair, but with the coming of spring I improved to crutches and a cot was placed at the back of our house so that I could hobble out and lie in the sunshine and air. "Nightfall" describes the approach of night as I witnessed here evening after evening, the "cows" being the only made-up touch that it contains.

THE FALL OF NIGHT

Here on the hill where cool winds blow
    I watch the day complete his quest
        And dusk from out the shadows rise.
Dusk lights her candles, row on row,
    And spreads her robes from east to west
        As lingering daylight fades and dies.
The silvery moon, a slender bow,
    Sinks down behind the mountain's crest,
        And night new-born rides up the skies.

Now night has come. The far-off heath
    Is still; and hushed are life's tired wails
        Scarce heard amid the day's mad sway.
Night lays upon the earth a wreath
    Of rest and drapes the skies in veils
        Of stars to recompense for day—
The same eternal stars beneath
    Which ancient sailors set their sails
        And ancient seers went out to pray.

The day imprisons us behind opaque walls of light, but the night opens our eyes to worlds beyond and frees our minds and spirits. Under a night sky, man found God and gave his first utterings on the meaning of things, and ever since, he has sought to enter through its portals into the mysteries of life and death. For night has been man's great teacher. By means of it he has discovered the laws of gravitation—laws so large that they reach unto the farthest star and hold it in place and so small that they control the fall of each tiny raindrop—and he believes that ultimately he will discover the whole of truth and, as master of it, build a new and better world.

In the winter of 1938–39, I made this the burden of a poem, which I began but never finished. I was working at Bakersville on a Government Works project, and rooming there, had my evenings free. Meditating on the influence of the night in contrast to that of the day on the knowledge and spiritual development of man, I began a poem on this subject, but when I got sick, in February of that winter, I had only the two stanzas comprising the introduction written. When my illness at length subsided until I could again think creatively my inspiration had passed, and not being able to get out under the stars that it might revive, I never finished it. However, I preserved the two stanzas since they were complete in themselves as a description of the fall of night.

Though my poem was to have been a thing of beauty it is just as well, I think, that it was never written. For since then I have had a change of attitude. I used to think that man—that is, the natural man (Homo sapiens as the evolutionists call him)—in his ageless quest after knowledge has discovered God. But now I know it was not truth that man wanted but power; God revealed Himself, but man wouldn't listen. I know also that it is not in man to direct his ways or build a better world, and that the knowledge he has piled up and calls truth is not truth but fable and must perish with him. For man—Homo sapiens—must perish, though he now rules the world, and his words with him; for otherwise God cannot fulfill His purpose to bring the earth to perfection and make of it a place of abode for His people, resurrected, regenerate man.

45

SECTION 5

Signs and Seasons

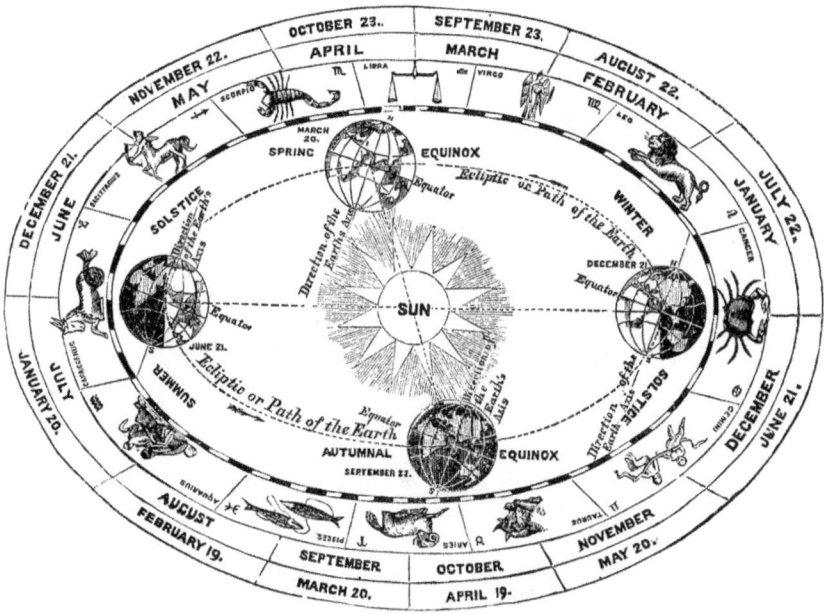

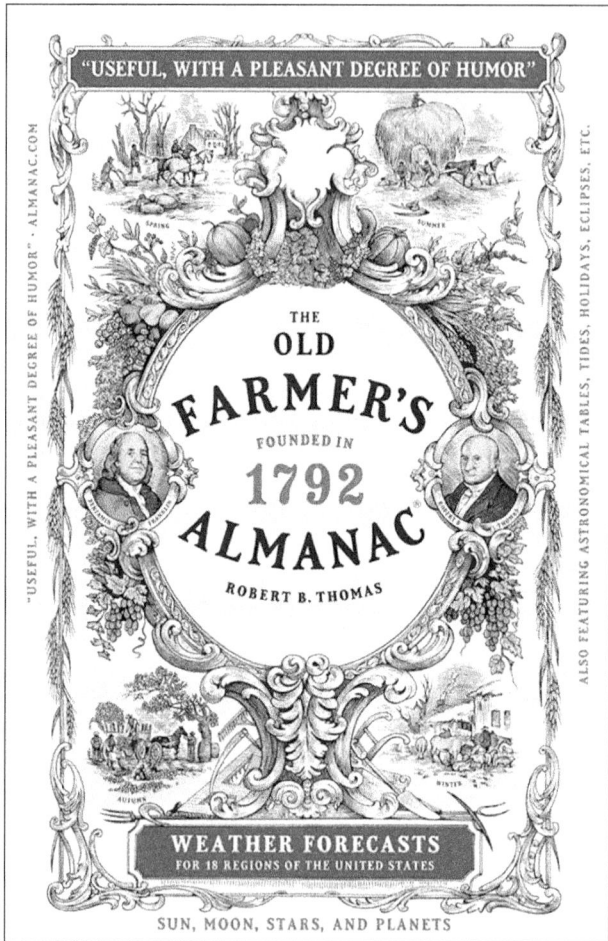

Used with permission from The Old Farmer's Almanac

The Signs and Seasons

Now the mountain people say in rhyme
That for everything there is a time,
And if as a farmer you'd succeed
Then the signs and seasons you must heed—
Supply yourself with an almanac
Or all your efforts'll go to rack,
And plant your seeds when the signs come right
If the moon is full and the nights are light.

For the signs, they say, with their symbols twelve
Were made for the folk who dig and delve.
In the form of a man in the almanac—
You'll find them shown in the front or back,
They start in the head and go out the feet,
Then rise and the downward trip repeat;
And each one rules in manifold ways
The mysteries of life through its quota of days.

You should plant, they say, when the signs are high,
If your patch is fixed and the weather's dry;
For the truth of the fact is widely felt
That the favored signs come above the belt.
Yet the mountain folk, they can show by test

That for certain things the others are best;

For the truth of the fact is also known

That everything's ruled by a sign of its own.

For cabbage as hard and heavy as lead

You must plant when the signs are up in the Head.

Then skipping the Neck, come down to the Twins

For your beans and corn if you want full bins.

And then is the time for melons and rue

Asparagus, peas, and cauliflowers too.

But travel you east or travel you west,

For onions and bulbs the sign is the Breast.

For onions and bulbs? The sign is the same

For watery cress and strawberries tame.

But come for your beets to the red, red Heart—

The purpose you'll see if you're clever and smart.

But for reasons of smell, the good wife howls

"Beware when the signs have come to the Bowels:

Plant not, nor pickle, nor make your kraut,

Till the signs from the Bowels have clean gone out!"

For 'taters the rule's to the piece three eyes

When the signs have dropped to the Reins or Thighs.

For turnips the rule's the same as for 'taters,

And the same applies to squashes and 'maters.

'Tis little, however, does well in the Knees

'Cept peppers and kale and black-eyed peas;

And ever'body knows that nothing ever grows

When the signs have come to the Feet and Toes.

Yet some folks claim that melons and vines

Belong to the lower bracket of signs;

And the housewives say not to set your eggs

Till the signs have passed from the Trunk to the Legs;

And the fishers add that beyond a doubt

The lower the signs the livelier the trout.

But it is as a rule by all conceded

That the moon and signs must both be heeded.

If wheat you're planning, then plan with care

And cast your seed when the moon shines fair—

Not when it's crooked and bent like a bow

Or you and the miller a begging will go.

And the same rule holds for your grass and clover

If a set you'd have when the winter's over

For the fathers say it was known of old
That crooked-moon plants won't stand the cold.

You should graft, they say, when the moon is new
For your grafts to knit and the sap push through.
And then is the time for to pick your ducks,
For old-moon feathers are dry like shucks.
But the old folks warn, if you want good wool,
Not to shear your sheep till the moon is full
Nor gather your herbs and wild-cherry bark
Till the moon is old and the nights are dark.

You must move, they say, when the moon is new
If you'd like to climb as the moon climbs too;
For he who moves when the moon's awane
Will gather no moss till he moves again.
But the mountain men warn, when you cover your shack,
Not to rive your boards when the nights are black;
For as sure, they say, as the morning mists
Your crooked-moon boards will warp up and twist.

Don't spread your manure when the moon is young
Or all summer long you'll grabble through dung,
Nor send for the man to change your shoats

Till the new moon's form as an old moon floats.
For manure that's spread when the moon is new
Won't mix with the soil the whole summer through,
And your pigs if changed when the moon is young
Will yield you no profit but squeals and dung.

Moreover, they warn, if the moon is thin,
Not to kill your hogs till the full moon's in;
Nor plant your corn when the moon's a bow,
Or the stalks as tall as the moon will grow.
For ever'body knows that thin-moon meat
Hain't fit for the cats and dogs to eat;
And ever'body says, though the signs are right,
Not to plant your corn till the moon shines bright.

For it sometimes happens, given good weather,
That the moon and signs don't come together;
And when such is the case, by faith or by test,
You must decide which time is the best.
For most of the folks in the matter versed
Contend for the one or t'other as first,
But a few maintain that neither is wrong
And one is as broad as t'other is long.

Now these are the rhymes of the mountain folk

Who follow the signs their fathers spoke,

And if as a farmer you'd succeed

Then their wit and wisdom you should heed—

Supply yourself with an almanac

To keep informed of the zodiac;

And plant your seeds when the signs come right,

If the moon is full and the nights are light.

"The Signs and Seasons," my longest rhymed poem, was written after my last illness began. It is not quite a picture of contemporary rural mountain life—modern roads and schools have seen to that—but it is almost; until a generation ago we were ruled in every phase of our life by the signs, and had been from times immemorial. From community to community there was some variation in them, but since they all stemmed from the same source—the moon and the almanac—they were remarkably uniform. The poem gives the pattern as it existed in my community. I made up nothing, being merely the scribe and rhymester; the contents were lifted out of the hearts of the people.

This very long poem followed an equally long debate within the family about using astrological signs and phases of the moon in selecting when to plant and when to harvest, etc. In the Thomas family, the parents were firmly entrenched in the old way and no amount of logic or explanation could persuade them to change. Their position was steadfast, while the sons argued that such positions had no scientific evidence or merit.

MARY'S VISION

The stars sang out the tiding in the night
    When angels came to shepherds on a hill
And Wise-men of the east beheld a light,
    But to a lowly stall in Bethlehem
No heavenly visions winged their earthward flight.

Yet to the Virgin Mother of His Child
    God gave a vision sweeter than all these:
For lo, as morning gleamed across the wild
    A mother's vision in her heart was born
When in the manger Jesus waked and smiled.

That God sent tidings to others that first Christmas night but none to the young mother of His Son used to be a thing of great marvel to me. But not after I had thought on it. For God did send her a vision, a vision not borne of angels but born in her heart when she first looked into the face of her newborn Child and dreamed of His future. Surely He could not have sent her a greater vision than this, common to all motherhood, and the more I thought on it the greater it seemed. At length I decided to write a poem on it, and I did so in 1928, the year I taught at Hawk, while boarding at Mr. Reid's.

A New Year's Wish

O New Year, won't you pause tonight
    When out upon the hallowed air
You rise to start your newborn flight
    And hear a shut-in's humble prayer?

This is the wish I crave of you,
    The boon I beg you for my own:
A task to do when day is new,
    A task well done when day has flown.

January

Su	Mo	Tu	We	Th	Fr	Sa
					1	2
3	4	5	6	7	8	9
10	11	12	13	14	15	16
17	18	19	20	21	22	23
24	25	26	27	28	29	30
31						

To the New Year

New Year, you come attended by the snow

And the blinding northwest winds.

A cold countenance yours to make a request to!

But I know behind your icy stars there is a smile.

And that you will bring the spring.

New Year, down under the hill

A violet nestles her tender roots!

Oh, how I have loved it all,

Every hour of every day

And every day of all the year.

To arise with the flowers in the spring

And go with them through their summer growth

Until they are laid to sleep beneath the snow;

To know wind and rain and sunshine,

Day and night with all their aspects,

And every bush and rock and drop of dew—

These have been among the joys

That every hour of every day has distilled for me.

New Year, what I meant to ask is this:

If fate has ordained that these and I must part,

In the new life to which you take me

May I find somewhere a little spot of earth

Like the earth that I have known?

SECTION 6

Nature

EARTH'S FIRST SONG

Amazed, the angels hushed their harps of gold
And to the outer space their hearing lent:
There rose from lower depths a sweeter song
Than the Celestial Band had ever heard.
Their graceful forms o'er Heaven's border bent,
Across the great expanse their gaze they rolled,
And pierced the mighty void, and then along
A gleam their vision glided to the earth
Where, in a Garden bathed in evening dew
There sang for God His first-created bird.
The song, ascending, rose to higher birth—
Enrapt, the angels tuned their harps anew.

"Earth's First Song" was inspired, first, by a children's story in which an insignificant act on earth produced an eventful reaction in heaven; second, by my study of birds in which I was gladdened by the thought that they were God's first created singers, and saddened that of all His creation to which He gave the voice of song—bird and man in particular—only they continue to give him undivided glory; and third, by contemplating God walking in the cool of the evening in the Garden of Eden. How these three combined to give me the idea for the poem, I have forgotten—perhaps it was the thought that God still walks in the cool of the evening to enjoy the spontaneous praise of the birds—but I distinctly remember its writing; it was on a winter day in which I was kept indoors by a deep snow.

MOONLIGHT

Out in the night

Out in the moonlight

So enchanting

Here thoughts are free and glad

Some sweet and some sad

But all like thee, thou mystic Moon

Full of enchantment.

This little half-rhymed free verse was written in 1924 and was my second poem. How well I remember the night that called it out!

THE RAIN

Nature is still and sad, like a woman before tears come.

What she has done I know not,

But her song is hushed

And a great quietness steals over everything

As the low-lying clouds come up and cover the land

And hide her face from the light of the sun.

Not a bird stirs, not a twig moves or a leaf quivers,

And in the graying mists the birches, like young girls,

Hold up their slender limbs as if in supplication.

The clouds darken and hang low, the mists thicken,

And the gloom deepens and covers all.

Deepens, too, the gloom of my life—

Griefs for the pain and sorrows that have been and will be,

Coming down like the graying clouds and mists,

Covering and hiding my soul with darkness

And filling my heart with sadness.

Presently nature weeps.

Softly, silently, she weeps,

And through the rain come the glad, welling notes of a bird.

And to me, too, after a long while, come tears

And the soft, healing voice of a song.

To the Wood Thrush

If you, unknowing, God adore,
Should not I, knowing, serve Him more?
This thought was one among a train
Awakened by your sweet refrain
As through the woods you took your flight
And filled my soul with pure delight.
For sweeter strains or more sincere
It's never been my joy to hear
Than pours from you, my gifted friend,
When evening's shadows fall and blend.

And oft when in the evening's cool
I seek the quiet of wood and pool,
I pause awhile beside the stream
And listen to your wildwood dream.
Like faery strains in visions fair
It swells upon the 'raptured air,
And wakes a chord within my soul
That seeks to reach a nobler goal.

First written in summer of 1927 but revised many times. My interest in birds was first awakened by my cousin, Mrs. Nolia Edwards, of Raleigh, who is a great lover of the outdoors. Visiting us in the summer of 1927, she taught me to distinguish many of the birds and their songs, and from that beginning my love of them has grown into a passion that has never abated. I have not learned much about their habits, true, but their music has opened a door into a new world of joy and beauty around me. It is a world, I have learned, not darkened with evil and sorrow like ours, but unrestrainedly happy and free, and still true to its created purpose of giving glory to God. For from these feathered citizens of the fields and woods there goes up more praise to Him than there does from us who are made in His likeness.

But of all the birds the thrush came to mean the most to me, perhaps because it was most in evidence at evening when I took my walks. Its song lifted me up out of the pettiness of my daily life and brought out the best that was in me. It meant so much to me that I felt impelled to write a poem to it, trying to put its meaning in the most beautiful words at my command lest I discredit the bird. I never succeeded as I hoped to, the last two lines of the first stanza being especially hard to bring to my meaning and liking. But what joy writing it gave me!

To the Wood Thrush, Again

Thou'rt pouring forth thy song with all thy might,

Thou gifted bird, thou happy wildwood sprite!

Thou surely hast in thee a spark divine,

Else where didst thou receive that song of thine,

Now loud and clear, now tremulous and low?

Or hast thou lived in ages long ago,

And is thy song some lover's happy dream

Sung on the flowery bank of sylvan stream?

A May Morning

How glad and thankful the growing things are!
Last night the rains came
And wet the ground and cooled the air
And gave the thirsting plants and grass and flowers
A drink of life.
This morning one can almost see and hear them grow
As they seek to outdo themselves
In their gladness.
Every briar and bush and weed is stretched up to its full
        height and glory,
Every leaf and blade of grass is spread out to its full width,
And those violets hold up their heads in gratitude
To a sky that's washed so clean it's as blue
As a pair of new overalls,
While that catbird perched among those half-grown leaves
Lets his breakfast go by
That he may publish how good it is to be alive
On this fine May morning.

"A May Morning" was not made up out of my head, but is a true description of an actual morning in May, which came not many years ago. There had been ten days to two weeks of very dry, hot weather and then one night when no one expected it but everybody wanted it there came a drenching downpour of rain. The next morning when I went out I found nature exactly as I reported it—washed, clean, and joyous, and in all the exuberance of life that comes after a refreshing rain following a hot dry spell.

SONG

Come, pretty maid, you were not made for tears,
      Come, we'll hie us to the fair green hills,
Where you will soon forget your griefs and fears.
      Heed not the aged voices calling,
But come, we'll haste away with break of day
      To the wooded vales and rippling rills,
Where on a moss-lined bank we'll dance and play
      Till evening's dusky shades come falling,
      Come away, pretty maid, come away.

Come, pretty maid, while still the years are young,
      Come, we'll hie us the fair green hills
Of joy, for youth's a song that soon is sung,--
      Thereafter's time enough for weeping.
The mosses cry, "Pretty maid, do not stay!"
      The sweet rills call, the sweet-purling rills,
With thoughts of love, "Come away, come away
      To the fair green hills the vales are keeping."
      Come away, pretty maid, come away.

I once heard a farmer skilled in the use of herbs say that he believed nature hold a cure for every bodily ill we suffer from; and while I cannot vouch for the truth of his conclusion I do believe that nature holds healing for all our spiritual ills if we would but seek it. At least, I have found it so as regards myself. Whether I have been troubled with strife, petty annoyances, grief, or spiritual unbalance, until my last illness cut me off, I could always find healing in nature; and no teas or other concoctions were to brew, all I had to do was to go out into the fields and woods and nature did the rest. It was this healing I had in mind when I wrote "Come, Pretty Maid." I thought, in particular, of the thousands in cities who know not of the balm in nature, not even what nature is, and as I meditated, my reflection narrowed down to a single person, a pretty maiden, in grief, to whom I issued an appeal to come to the woods and be healed. The poem was hard to construct because of the difficult rhyme scheme I chose, the fourth line being especially hard. When it was finished, my brother, Walter, in college that summer in Boone, showed it to his English teacher, who read it and shook his head. He did not like it, he said, it was too Elizabethan. I hardly know whether to consider his objection as a fault or a compliment, but in the end I felt flattered. I had been reading Shakespeare that summer, and my mind was intoxicated with the haunting beauty of his lyrics.

To the Wild Rose

Mother Nature's purest child,

Thou'rt the thorny queen of nature's wild.

Thy color thine, thy odor sweet,

Thou'rt not for flowery gardens meet,

And when in wonder I had guessed

Why thou art not by man so blessed

These were the thoughts that came to me:

In goodness God created thee

For the wild bird and buzzing bee

And lowing herd upon the lea;

For nature's great and nature's small,

The good, the wayward, one and all,

And placed thee in a thorny lot

For all to see; for man is not

The only lover of true beauty.

The inspiration for "To a Wild Rose" came suddenly and unexpectedly one day several summers prior to the writing of "To the Wood Thrush." I had crawled up through a deep gully above our house at Lunday, exploring for minerals, when, reaching the head and finding none, I raised up and saw hanging over the bank above me the briar of a wild rose heavily laden with flowers. I was never so agreeably surprised in my life, for it was altogether unexpected, and getting out, I was overwhelmed by the loveliness of the flower in its wild setting and asked myself what was its meaning, hidden here alone instead of being in some man's yard? Like a flash the answer came, the first time that such a revelation had ever entered my mind, that beauty is not found in yards and flower gardens only, but is everywhere, created for every eye in nature, for the bird's, the ant's, and the bee's, as well as for man's. All the remainder of that week I walked in the clouds, meditating on this truth and resolving how to put it into a poem to the wild rose which had been the means of bringing it to me. Come Sunday and Sunday school and dinner at last over, I took my chair and pencil and paper, and going out under the shade of an apple tree, went to work. When supper was called I was surely the happiest person in Lunday, for my poem was finished and my joy was unbounded. Many who have read my poems think it my finest, and my cousin, Mrs. Edwards, liked it so well that she named her little girl, born soon after it was written, jointly after it and her mother, calling her Rosemary. This is the greatest honor I have ever received from any of my poems.

WILD ROSES

Frail, fragrant, pale-red wild roses!

Growing in rocky places, among scrubby bushes, beside
thorny hedges;

Living intimately with nature, the sun, the moon, and the
stars, the fogs, the rains, and the dews;

Blooming in the long balmy days of June, ladening the
evenings and mornings with delicate perfume,

Diffusing their redolent odors over the wild hills to the
grazing cattle, the bumblebees, the butterflies, and
the birds;

Receding from man with his changing hands, losing their
beauty, purity, sweetness under the hands of
cultivation.

More beautiful than gentians, forget-me-nots,
honeysuckles; sweeter than violets, lilies, and their
sisters the tame roses.

Beloved of poets, children, and the lovers of nature;
symbols of love, innocence, freedom;

Frail, fragrant, pale-red wild roses!

---

*I dare say "Wild Roses" could hardly be called a poem but is instead a
by-product consisting of trimmings from my poem, "To the Wild Rose."
I included it to show how one in writing a poem sees much more than he
actually puts in the poem. The finished product can contain only the central
thought of his musings, a view framed by a very small window. But to be
a good poem it must be so constructed as to arouse the reader to the same
meditations from which it came.*

FALL

The valleys below are black;
But the mountains,
Shrouded in the veil of the first snow,
Stand out like gray tombstones
In the somber night.
With their icy breath they chill my frame
And cast depression into my soul,
For they are mute omens
Of the bleak winter.

"Fall" was written while I was in teacher training, as an assignment in our course in composition. I had poems which I could have used, which my classmates and instructor knew nothing about, but thinking it unfair to do so, I decided to write a new one and began casting about in my mind for a subject. But none offered itself and still had not when the last day before the assignment was due arrived and drew toward a close. That evening, coming home on the school bus, which was late, I tried to look at every house differently, hoping for inspiration, but all to no purpose. A raw, cloudy evening in early November, when the bus arrived at the top of the hill above our house and disgorged us, a chill wind cut me to the bone, and glancing dejectedly toward the horizon, I was struck by the contrast between the mountains, white with the first snow, and the valley below, black in the gathering dusk. It was a picture deeply ominous of winter, a season I dreaded that year, having to ride the bus, and as I contemplated it depression seized me. But suddenly I was raised to the heights, for like a flash, inspiration for the wanted poem leaped into my mind, born of the scene before me. When I reached home it was finished, all but the title which my instructor Mrs. Gouge supplied the next day. The praise she and my classmates gave it completed my joy.

Burn, Kindly Fire

Burn, kindly fire, burn, warmly burn.
  Outside the cold winds howl and blow
And every leaf and twig and fern
  Lies deeply hid beneath the snow.

Burn, kindly fire, burn, brightly burn!
  And fill our room with cheerful glow
While every leaf and twig and fern
  Lies deeply hid, and cold winds blow.

THE ANSWER

I

At dusk the trees were ghostly black and bare,

As Nature, wan, sighed through the hazy air;

     She thought their loveliness was marred in nudity:

I heard her kneel and softly breathe a prayer.

II

At dawn the trees no more were dark and sere,

But richly dressed in raiment rare and dear;

     For God had heard and sent an answer in the night:

A lovely snow adorned them far and near.

As in all of my nature poems, "The Answer" is based on an actual experience. At the end of a cloudy day I went out alone to walk, and everything, it seemed to me, was saddened by the gloomy bareness of the landscape, now nude in the midst of winter, and especially by that of the trees, ghostly in the dusk. I imagined Nature, personified, sighing up and down the valley and at last kneeling in prayer that the trees and plants, her visible body, might be clothed. The next morning a miracle had happened, a lovely snow had covered the landscape with raiment rare and dear. We expected it, of course, but I fancied that Nature did not; it was an unexpected answer to her prayer. With a rapturous heart I wrote my poem that day, seeking only to bring out the beauty of the scene and leaving the lesson for the reader to infer or pass by. For God can clothe with white raiment a soul blackened with sin just as suddenly as He changed the face of nature that night. But the change must come through prayer.

Life and Death

THE LEGEND OF DEATH HOLE

There is a tangled wood in a bend of the creek between the mill and the church in our community,

And in the midst of the wood there rises perpendicularly from one side of the creek a massive gray rock,

Above which, back where the soil begins, there lies a single unmarked grave,

And below which there swirls down in the creek a deep hole of dark winding waters

That is feared and shunned by all the community's fisher-boys.

One morning a long time ago, legend says, strange howling noises began coming out of this hole—

Weird, mysterious howlings like the anguished wails of a wild beast caught and made desolate—

And the same day a spell came over Wilson Powell and he went down and drowned himself in its waters.

He was 80-odd years old, a patriarch loved and respected by all, and nobody knew why he committed suicide,

But the hole suddenly hushed its howling and the people said that a spirit lived imprisoned in it,

That the weird, mysterious noise was its message to him, understood by him and him alone,

And that his death was his answer.

The next day all his kith and kin and all the people went down and got long poles and rescued his body.

And they brought it up out of the waters and buried it in an unhallowed spot of ground above the rock.

And after that they called the place Death Hole and said that if ever it began howling again it'd take its victim.

And fear and trembling came upon them and for many years they lived and moved in apprehension,

But when the years came and went and nothing ever happened they lost their fear and dread,

And the superstition mellowed into a legend with which mothers frightened their children.

That is the sum and end of the legend of Death Hole as handed down to us by our fathers.

A few years ago, however, there came a stranger into our community, a visitor from a northern state,

Who was much impressed with the legend of Death Hole and got the people to tell it to him over and over,

And he asked many questions about the legend and went down and visited the place and made notes and took pictures.

Then he passed on, and seeing him no more we soon forgot about him and his curiosity.

But last year there came by chance a book of folklore tales into our community,

A book of folklore tales of the southern mountains written by this same man,

Although he had passed himself among us as a tired office worker seeking rest,

And in it he told the story of Death Hole.

He gave the beginning and body of the legend truthfully, and with great beauty and tenderness,

But instead of closing with the real ending, the ending which I have given you and the one that he was told,

He made up and ending of his own, a scene without any factual or folklore basis whatsoever,

And gave it as the way in which the legend really closed.

The superstition, he said, continued to be a living fear in the lives of the people,

And that one Christmas eve not many years ago while all were out making merry,

Death Hole began howling again—a low, ominous howling that filled the valley with its awful fulfillment,

And froze the hearts of the people with fear as they fled from the places of their merriment

And sought the shelter of their homes, where behind barred doors and drawn shades

They huddled in terror the long night through.

But when morning came and they unfastened their doors and went out

Death Hole had mysteriously hushed

And a young woman, the comeliest and most popular in all the community, was missing.

Tracking her through the new-fallen snow, he said, they came in sorrow down to Death Hole,

And following the footmarks upon the rock, they stopped, for there down in the dark winding waters

Swirled her beautiful half-clad body, a sacrifice to that awful summons which they had all heard,

But which she and she alone had understood and answered.

And now, he concluded, two lonely unmarked graves lie in silent vigil above the rock,

And in the dusk of the evening the people gather in their homes and wonder in hushed voices

Which one of them will be called when Death Hole howls again…

Suddenly a legend which the people had always loved and been proud of turned sour in their minds

When the burden of it superstition was shifted so as to fall on them as well as on their fathers,

And they said that it was a bad out that it couldn't have been left in the past where it belonged,

And if it had to be told, told as it was and without some-body's made-up piece stuck on to it.

But the point I wish to make in all this is, that with most of us it is awfully hard

Not to overtell a good tale.

THE RACE

Last night I raced

Adown the fields of time

With Death.

The prize: my breath. I won,

But Death, not I, wore the victor's gloat.

For Death knows that I have no choice

But to race whenever he bids

And that sooner or later the victory will be his.

CRUDE MARKINGS ON A STONE

                    Today I found
A woodland stone whereon a lover long
Ago had carved, in markings crude, his and
His loved one's names, linked by a heart. Time passed.
The maid, perhaps deceived, had come again and graved
Her curse below. Thus wrote those lovers two,
Who many years have lain beneath the grasses,
Little dreaming they had left their marks
Upon the face of time.
                    So are our lives.
We live our little day and then are gone.
We think, but 'tis not so. On everyone
We meet we leave our marks: a smile, a tear,
A joy, a wound that will not heal—crude marks
And smooth, which cycling down the years live on
Long after we in mortal flesh are dead.

"Crude Markings on a Stone," my first unrhymed poem, was inspired by a tree seen in childhood with letterings cut into its bark, which to later suit my purposes, I changed to a stone. This is one of my few poems in which I attempted to teach a lesson. The parallel between the crude markings of the lovers and our own unconscious markings on the lives of all we come into contact with impressed me very much, and I could not refrain from pointing out the moral. I hope the reader will not think it overdrawn, for an overdrawn moral is worse than no moral at all. The most difficult construction in this poem was the writing of the last two lines of the first stanza, the tense of the verbs occasioning it.

DEATH OF THE MOUNTAIN MAN

He wore mean raiment, rose with morning's rise,
      And toiled till day no more of light could give
From youth to age, through pain and sacrifice,
      That he a more abundant life might live.
But ere he came his bounds and ends were wrought;
      He never reached the place he hoped to fill;
Board and bed were all his wages ever bought;
      And all he ever owned, a stony plot to till.

Now he is dead, think you he toiled in vain?
      Think you the goal, the ever-onward must
Toward which he strove, and ever hoped to gain,
      With mortal flesh lies ashes in the dust?
Think you he's dead and gone for evermore,
      And pain the only crown he ever wore?

---

*Written on a bleak winter day in 1938, when they came and told me,
"Stokes Buchanan is dead."*

In Heaven

In heaven

I will not ask for a harp;

But growing tired,

Will steal out from the angel throng

And wander on alone

Until I find a wooded hill

With singing birds and wild flowers

And a rock or a mossy log

Whereon to sit and dream

Until the sun listing down the west

Brings the night with a silvery moon

Or the friendly stars.

This poem has been attacked on the ground that it fails to show a proper appreciation of the things God has prepared for those who love Him, but I think it shows the very height of appreciation since we must first learn to appreciate what God has given us here before we can have any surety that we will appreciate what lies beyond. And one of the greatest things He has given us is a love of solitude, that being away from man but with God and nature.

POSTSCRIPT

Monroe Thomas died on February 10, 1957, and his remains lie next to his parents in the Kona Silver Cemetery. In addition to his poems, he produced copious writings on topics he found useful and interesting, including a lengthy treatise on community-based education. He also maintained detailed journals outlining family farming practices and the daily goings-on in his community.

His last journal entry is dated June 23, 1956 in which he describes an illness that his long time friend and doctor, Dr. Gouge, diagnosed as anemia. Monroe agreed with the superficial diagnosis, but he questioned its cause and added, "whatever it is, is lapping up my blood faster than my body can make it." Monroe's suspicion of an underlying cause was justified by a later diagnosis of leukemia, and in retrospect, it had its genesis in the disease that had plagued him since childhood. His immune system had fought a long and valiant defense against the infection of osteomyelitis, but in doing so, it had been forced to make many more immune cells and undergo many more cell divisions than normal. With each new division, the probability of a mistake in the control of unleashed multiplication occurred, and finally, the immune cell division increased to levels that began to overwhelm the number of oxygen carrying blood cells, thus leading to anemia and leukemia as the precipitating cause.

Even after he had reluctantly given up writing in his journal, he composed long letters in answer to inquiries about the Silver family. In one of these he notes that he "now spends most of my time lying down" but he was still valiantly writing!

His niece, Jo Ann Thomas Croom, is working on other compilations of his work, as well as the stories written by her father, Walter, about growing up on a mountain farm in the early 1900s. She hopes to combine these and the journal writings of Monroe into a historical account of this part of the Appalachian region. This was a time of dramatic change for the community and the family, recorded in real time by two brothers who were both historians and educators.

www.ingramcontent.com/pod-product-compliance
Lightning Source LLC
LaVergne TN
LVHW051422080426
835508LV00022B/3196